ISBN 978-1-333-34373-6
PIBN 10493049

This book is a reproduction of an important historical work. Forgotten Books uses
state-of-the-art technology to digitally reconstruct the work, preserving the original format
whilst repairing imperfections present in the aged copy. In rare cases, an imperfection in
the original, such as a blemish or missing page, may be replicated in our edition. We do,
however, repair the vast majority of imperfections successfully; any imperfections that
remain are intentionally left to preserve the state of such historical works.

1 MONTH OF
FREE
READING

at

www.ForgottenBooks.com

By purchasing this book you are eligible for one month membership to ForgottenBooks.com, giving you unlimited access to our entire collection of over 1,000,000 titles via our web site and mobile apps.

To claim your free month visit:

www.forgottenbooks.com/free493049

English
Français
Deutsche
Italiano
Español
Português

www.forgottenbooks.com

Mythology Photography **Fiction**
Fishing Christianity **Art** Cooking
Essays Buddhism Freemasonry
Medicine **Biology** Music **Ancient
Egypt** Evolution Carpentry Physics
Dance Geology **Mathematics** Fitness
Shakespeare **Folklore** Yoga Marketing
Confidence Immortality Biographies
Poetry **Psychology** Witchcraft
Electronics Chemistry History **Law**
Accounting **Philosophy** Anthropology
Alchemy Drama Quantum Mechanics
Atheism Sexual Health **Ancient History**
Entrepreneurship Languages Sport
Paleontology Needlework Islam
Metaphysics Investment Archaeology
Parenting Statistics Criminology
Motivational

THE LAST
SCRATCH OF AN
OCTOGENARIAN
PEN

THE LAST SCRATCH

OF

AN OCTOGENARIAN PEN.

BY

ROBERT NEEDHAM CUST, LL.D.

HERTFORD

PRINTED BY STEPHEN AUSTIN AND SONS.

———

1903.

THE LAST SCRATCH OF AN OCTOGENARIAN PEN,

SEPTEMBER, 1903, AGED 83.

THE idea of a Series of Volumes, containing reprints of Essays, and small Volumes, was suggested by my own experience. I have gleaned a great deal of knowledge from contributions to Periodicals: in course of time the author dies, the name of the periodical is forgotten, and I have been unable after a lapse of twenty years to refer to the contribution, as no one can recollect where or when it appeared. To obviate this in my own case I arranged to reprint all my contributions to Periodicals, of which there are scores, and all Pamphlets and small Volumes, in my Seven Series of Linguistic and Oriental Essays.

But this is not enough. I have found people asking for a writing of mine written forty years ago, and it gave me much trouble to find it. So I have now compiled Three Lists (see p. 369 et seq.):

I. Chronological List of Writings : this contains a record of everything that I have put into print, or retained in Manuscript Volumes, 1,270 in number.

II. List of Separate Volumes, 60 in number. Of these last a great many are sold out, or entirely given away.

III. List of Books of which copies are still to be obtained, prepared up to date by the Printer, in whose charge all the books are.

It is with a mixed feeling of joyful gratitude and pain that I contemplate the Chronological List of my Writings during the seventy years which have passed since 1834, when at the age of 13 at Eton College I first handled the pen; and in my 83rd year I am unwillingly wiping it dry and putting it down. My work in life is done, and I have had a good time of it, as the List shows, as it has 1,270 entries recorded. In addition there are several Quarto Volumes of Cuttings from different Newspapers in

Great Britain, or India, or some other Country, and a great number of Manuscript Volumes of different dates.

A wise man was once asked to express an opinion as to the comparative pleasure of the Composer of a new Book, and the Parent of a new Baby. After careful thought he replied that the birth of a new Baby gives greater pleasure at the time, but causes infinite expense, and trouble, and possibly annoyance, for the rest of the Parent's life; while the birth of the Book is attended with infinite trouble at the time, but causes no expense, or trouble, or annoyance, afterwards, and possibly may bring in profit to the Parent. The birth of both Book and Baby seems to be a matter of absolute chance, and there is no limitation in either case as to age, as I am putting forth my Sixtieth Volume at the age of 82, while a brother Magistrate of the County of London is indulging himself in an annual Baby at the same age, and it is quite uncertain, whether in either case the latest birth will be the last.

I was at Eton College when I caught the *cacoethes scribendi*, or the infection of Composition in Prose and Verse in Latin and Greek, which formed then the chief part of our Education, accompanied by weekly repetition of passages from Latin and Greek Poets, or the study in the Class-room of Prose-writers. I suppose that this was the way in which the disease, which has clung to me for a long life, was caught, and the motive was purely voluntary, as I never wrote a line for the sake of profit, and if in some cases money came from the sale of printed matter, it went to pay the expense in part of the Printers' Bill, and as I grew older and stronger I deliberately gave away hundreds of volumes of my books on Missions or a Scientific Subject. I used to send forty copies of each Series of Linguistic and Oriental Essays to Libraries of Great Britain, the same number to Libraries in the United States, ten copies to Libraries in India, and ten to Libraries on the Continent. Add to this an unlimited supply of copies to friends and acquaintances, and men of Science. And in return I received profuse thanks, and presentation Volumes of the recipients' books. I must here relate two anecdotes.

I had occasion at the Bodleian Library, Oxford, to hunt for a Book, which I wished to consult. My eye was attracted by my own name in the list of Authors, and I found three or four large sheets of the Register covered with the names of my Publications.

On another occasion I was at Stockholm, and I called in at the Library to inquire whether they had any new Books on the Languages of Africa. "Yes," was the reply, "and an excellent Book of the kind," and the Librarian produced my own two-volumed Book on the Languages of Africa, which had just appeared in London. I seemed to feel in both these cases a new idea of the pleasure of Fame.

I contributed Articles for fifty years to a great number of Periodicals; for instance, to the *Calcutta Review* I sent fifty-three contributions, and the same number to the Journal of the Royal Asiatic Society. And as time went on and I found that there was an undistributed stock of copies of my Book in the hands of my Printers, I used to send out a copy of this Circular, and got a large number into circulation. I mention this to encourage other Authors to do the same.

" DEAR SIR,
" I submit to your notice a Memorandum of the copies of
" books published by me at my own cost, which I have still in
" store.
" If you have any desire to possess any of these books, which
" were printed, not for profit, but for the purpose of diffusing my
" views on certain subjects, I should be happy to present you with
" copies, free of cost, if you will apply to my Printer.
" A good many of my books have been entirely disposed of, and
" are omitted from this list."

Some readers may not appreciate the difference between a Book, and an Essay, but it is this: a Book, like the great glories of past Centuries, consists often of many Volumes, while an Essay is only part of a Volume; as time goes on it forms part of a Volume, losing its identity as an Essay and becoming a Chapter of a great work. But it so happened that my studies and experiences were such, that if an Essay had not been written at the time, by stealing a few hours from the ceaseless burden of official business, it would have lost its freshness, or perhaps never have been written at all. And then it happens that some Essays will not coalesce with others in a Volume, so the device in my case of a Series of Linguistic and Oriental Essays was had recourse to; and when one Series had reached several hundred pages, another was opened, and a vast number of Contributions to Reviews, separate Pamphlets, and Articles in Newspapers were thrown together, and saved from the waters of Lethe, and published in such a form that they could find their way to the New as well as the Old World.   Then there often happens to be a variety of Languages, and some Volumes contain papers in English, French, German, Italian, Spanish, Greek, and my dear Hindustani : written in English by myself, and translated by competent scholars under my careful supervision, and proofreading.

Another feature of the Essay is, that after a lapse of years it recalls thoughts and feelings of bygone times.   I quote two Essays from my pen, which I wrote nearly forty years ago in a moment of deep depression, when by the will of God my prosperous career in India was brought to a sudden close, when I was cut off from official Honours, and, what I valued more, Usefulness, and crept back to my Native Land with my great Mission uncompleted. A kind friend said to me at the time that "Life was a period of compensations : if you do not get one thing, you get another." I have found it to be so, and have had nearly forty years of Usefulness, Literary employment, and Happiness.

"Diem perdidi."

Thanks are due to the glorious old heathen, who uttered these memorable words.   No doubt, in the discharge of his Imperial duties, he had that day issued orders to his Proconsuls in every part of the Roman World ; he had replied to the queries of his Generals, who commanded his scattered forces on the Euphrates, the Danube, and in distant Britain ; he had received the Ambassadors of Sovereigns, who held their sceptres at his pleasure ; he had given his sanction to new and wise laws regulating the affairs of the human race (as it appeared to him); he had worshipped devoutly at the altars of his country's gods ; he had presided at the games in the Flavian Amphitheatre, and entertained the nobles of Rome at a banquet on the Palatine : he seemed in the eyes of his courtiers to have done a good day's work, and yet when, according to the golden precepts of Pythagoras, he counted up what he had done, or left undone, before he closed his eyes in sleep, he felt, and he exclaimed aloud, with so deep an intonation that his words still ring in the hearts of men, that *he had lost a day.* He remembered, that he had on that day done no act of kindness ; had said no word of mercy, consolation, and love ; had devised no scheme of benevolence and charity ; had forgiven no personal injury ; had returned good for no evil; had alleviated no life of sorrow, want, and disappointment ; had by timely advice held back no rash spirit from the precipice of destruction ; had by judicious suggestion turned into a happier and more hopeful channel the jaundiced thought of no broken-hearted one ; had not ministered to any of the wants of his fellow-creatures ; he had not helped to bear the burden of any brother, and thus fulfil the great law of his own life : and so the great Emperor, clothed in purple, sighed, because he had lost a day. We think, that his memory was bad, and that probably he had done much, but his inner consciousness was moved, that he had not done enough. Verily, of such men, who are thus moved, is the Kingdom of Heaven.

Life is like a basket, which everyone must fill before night : let us put in something that is really good, and be not content to exclude what is absolutely bad ; something besides official reports, social conventionalities, and trivial amusements ; let us put in what is really good at once, for the night comes on apace, and the golden opportunity may be gone. The poor man may have moved on from our door with his wants unrelieved ; the sick man may have died with his bedside unvisited ; the neighbour, who might have been saved, may have erred beyond hope of recovery ; Christ Himself, in the form of a poor starving child, may have stood at our door and knocked, and not have been admitted ? Do we ever ask ourselves, as the long tedious hours of the Indian Summer day at length wear themselves out, " Have I done anything, tried to do anything, said anything, thought anything, for the good of my fellow-creatures, and for the Glory of my Saviour ? " No need to aspire to great things : little things make up the sum of life's history, and we are all capable of little things, so wisely typified in the cup of cold water, and the opportunity occurs so often, and in such multiform variety. We allude to the timely alms, the earnest co-operation, the word, only a word, of sympathy, the tribute of respect shown to unfashionable merit and goodness ; the manful standing up

against error even in high places, and to the probable detriment of
the opposer; the resistance to the current of down-grade morality,
low religion, low sense of public duty; the word of advice spoken
just in time to save; the thought wrought out which is able to
breathe new life to others; the words put to paper, which will
bring tears to the eyes, or burn the cheek of the reader, long after
you are slumbering in your grave. Let each of us do each day
something of this kind, or better, and he will not have lost a day;
his labour will not be in vain in the Lord, and his works will
follow him.

"*Southern Cross*," *Allahabad*, 1867.

So be it!

"In Te, Domine, speravi."

Changes of the most afflicting nature constantly occur in the circle
of our Anglo-Indian community with a suddenness and bitterness
which are quite appalling. We look around, and those, who were
our every-day companions, are gone. We hear of neighbours, young
and old, struck down by death, by disease, or incapacitated by
blindness, or crushed by such bereavements, as carry with them all
the bitterness, without the rest of death to the survivors. The air
is indeed filled with farewells of the dying, and wailings for the
dead; the casual acquaintance is disturbed by the complaints of
the broken-hearted, and the burden of the disappointed, and we
seem relieved, when the train carries off into space, no more to be
heard of, the member of the community, who has ceased to be
agreeable or useful. The turn of all comes, one by one; some
sooner, some later; some oftener, some at long intervals: the same
trite, well-meaning, but meaningless, consolation is tendered in all
cases, whether on the death of an infant of a few weeks, of an aged
parent, or one who hoped, and was hoped to be, the loving partner
of a long life. The only real consolation is contained in the words
we have above quoted, "Lord, in Thee have I trusted." Trust in
God always!

The path, which we have selected, may appear to be a promising
one for God's work, and a useful one and an agreeable one; but
a wall is suddenly found, which interrupts onward progress. The
heart sinks at the prospect of abandoning schemes of usefulness,

labours of love, prospects of success, brightened by loving sympathy, hallowed by sweet companionship. If God's service be our real object, let us not be cast down. Whether the impediment be sickness, bereavement, or disappointment, the Lord will provide for the sacrifice in His own time and in His own place. Let our hearts only be ready. Or the path, into which we have strayed, may be one of thoughtlessness, if not sin; of levity, if not an entire forgetfulness of God's service; of undue devotion to the world, and its honours and its snares, and a too eager gathering of the treasures, which perish, or clog when obtained. Let us be thankful, if a lion obstruct such a path, and let us welcome the calamity, whatever it may be, as God's Messenger, believing that our travel is afflicted with such trouble, lest the delight (over-delight of the provisions of the journey) should take away our desire for the Rest, which should be the journey's end. In such dark hours Trust in the Lord!

This is the last echo of a voice, or rather of two voices (one has been silent for three months in the grave, and the other will be heard here no more), which have striven to rouse their friends by advice, by illustration, by narratives, to a sense of a higher life, a nobler vocation, an obligation laid upon the British in India, to do something, each of us according to his ability, in the cause of our fellow-creatures, especially as regards spreading the Gospel among the people of India. The ardent desire to serve God here, longer and better, has not been gratified; but the sphere alone has been changed, *and not the work.* We may humbly believe, that the blessed saints, and spirits of the just made perfect, have still a work of Love and Self-sacrifice to do in their Father's Kingdom on high, and in the presence of that Saviour, whose faithful service was the Law of their brief mortal life. And the sufferer, left for a season to fill up the measure of his sufferings alone, will surely in due time find a work to be done by him below, if his Faith remains unshaken, and if he trusts in the Lord.

"*Southern Cross,*" *Allahabad, Nov.,* 1867.

So indeed, and more also, I have found it.

London, 1890.

Words uttered one day are forgotten next day, but if leisure permitted the sentiments which these words conveyed to the ear to be recorded on paper, something remains, which may have been

profitable to casual readers of the Volume, to read, and which after
the lapse of thirty-six years it is pleasant to think that someone
had grace to write it. It was written at Allahabad, my last residence
in India, and the date shows that it was written early in 1867, the
last year of my Indian life: perhaps it illustrates one of the ad-
vantages of contributing to the passing Literature of Periodicals.

Another reason why it is more easy and profitable to strike off
articles for Periodicals than to work at a great book on one subject
in many Volumes, like "The Decline and Fall of the Roman
Empire," by Gibbon. Some subject comes before you, which has
to be what is technically called got up by careful study, the con-
sulting of many books, or the visit of distant places. The best way
to utilize and perpetuate the acquired knowledge is by striking off
an Essay on the subject, while you have the materials under your
hand. This fact, or rather necessity, gave birth to a large number
of the Essays or Magazine Articles enumerated in the Catalogue.

In the India Civil Department there is necessarily an abundance
of writing of Reports from the official in charge of a District, or
a cluster of Districts known as a Division, and his superior officers.
They are necessarily long, but some officers acquire the art of not
making them tedious, and tell their story fully and intelligibly; and
great Administrators like Lord Lawrence, though perhaps they did
not possess the gift themselves, appreciated it in such subordinates
as Sir Richard Temple, and others.

In the administration of a newly conquered Province such as the
Panjáb in Northern India in 1844–1864, there was room for the
composition of many official Books in English or Urdu, and their
publication at the expense of the Government, Books which would
appear very odd in a list of Publications in England, but which had
their merit and use in India, and the Annual Reports of the Adminis-
trator of a Province taught the Compiler a lesson in the Art, and
many Members of the India Civil Service are famous for their
power of writing, while they have little or no power of public
speaking, as the mouth is not opened, and men are generally
what their environment makes them. I submit a list of my Indian
official Compositions: dull reading enough.

In another Essay I have described my Travels and Tours in
Europe, Asia, and Africa. Before such an excursion I used to
prepare myself by reading up all about the Country to be visited,

and after my return to my home, whether in India or England, a descriptive paper sent to some Periodical was the necessary conclusion.

Fifty years have elapsed since in 1850 I visited the Vale of Cashmere, then little known, and in 1851 I traversed Palestine, and after the lapse of half a Century, I read with delight my narrative of those delightful Tours. Other Essays record some Administrative experiences in my own Province of India, or describe the great Battles, in which I was present in 1845 and 1846, the result of which was the Conquest of the Panjáb, or brought into order the internal history of Languages, or some other delightful subject, which thrust itself under my observation twenty or forty years ago, and which formed the basis at a later date of some substantial Treatise. Poetry intermixed itself with Prose. My interest in Missions to Evangelize the Heathen led to the composition of many a Religious Essay, or Volume, and I am humbly thankful in my old age to think that I had Grace given to study the subject.

> " As by our works alone we shall be known,
> " We must not live to please ourselves alone ;
> " For Life's short space is lent for toil, and then
> " Love to our God, Love to our fellow-men.
> " When hundreds fell around on battlefield,
> " Thou o'er my head didst spread Thy gracious shield ;
> " And when in Peace the fell assassin's blow
> " My Chief, and my Subordinate, struck low,
> " I stood unharmed : and so it seems to me,
> " Serving my fellow-creatures I serve Thee."

R. N. Cust : *Poems of Many Years and Many Places*
(Second Series, p. 270).